# Helen
# Keller

A Buddy Book
by
Christy DeVillier

## ABDO
## Publishing Company

## VISIT US AT

**www.abdopub.com**

Published by ABDO Publishing Company, 4940 Viking Drive, Suite 622, Edina, Minnesota
55435. Copyright © 2004 by Abdo Consulting Group, Inc. International copyrights reserved
in all countries. No part of this book may be reproduced in any form without written
permission from the publisher.

Printed in the United States.

Edited by: Michael P. Goecke
Contributing Editor: Matt Ray
Image Research: Deborah Coldiron
Graphic Design: Jane Halbert
Cover Photograph: Library of Congress
Interior Photographs/Illustrations: Hulton Archives, North Wind

### Library of Congress Cataloging-in-Publication Data

Devillier, Christy, 1971-
    Helen Keller / Christy Devillier.
        v. cm. — (First biographies)
    Includes bibliographical references and index.
    Contents: Who is Helen Keller?—Growing up—Alexander Graham Bell
—Anne Sullivan—Teaching Helen—Going to college—Fame for Helen—An inspiration.
    ISBN 1-59197-514-X
    1. Keller, Helen, 1880-1968—Juvenile literature. 2. Blind-deaf women—United States—
Biography—Juvenile literature. 3. Sullivan, Annie, 1866-1936—Juvenile literature.
    [1. Keller, Helen, 1880-1968. 2. Blind. 3. Deaf. 4. People with disabilities. 5. Women—
Biography. 6. Sullivan, Annie 1866-1936.] I. Title.

HV1624.K4D48 2004
362.4'1'092—dc22
[B]
                                                                    2003052261

# Table Of Contents

# Who Is Helen Keller?

Helen Keller was blind and deaf. Yet, she learned to read, write, and speak. Helen wrote many books about her life. She is also famous for helping other blind people. Helen Keller has won many awards for her achievements.

Helen Keller

# Growing Up

Helen Keller was born June 27, 1880. Her parents were Kate and Arthur Keller. They lived on a cotton plantation in Tuscumbia, Alabama.

One day, young Helen became very sick. She may have had scarlet fever. Helen got better. But her sight and hearing began to fail. Helen became blind and deaf. She was about two years old.

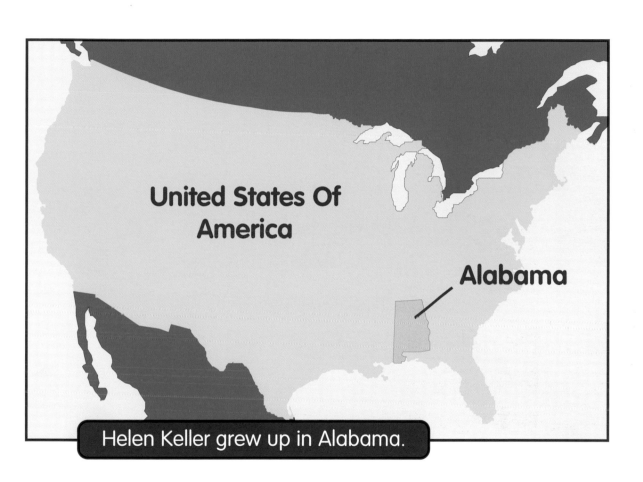

United States Of America

Alabama

Helen Keller grew up in Alabama.

# Alexander Graham Bell

Young Helen lived in a dark and quiet world. She could not speak to anyone. So, she began making signs with her hands. These signs helped people understand Helen. By age five, Helen used about 50 signs.

Young Helen was often angry and unhappy. Helen's parents were not sure how to help her. Helen's doctor said they should take Helen to Dr. Alexander Graham Bell. He had worked with deaf people. Dr. Bell was also famous for inventing the telephone.

Dr. Alexander Graham Bell and Helen became good friends.

Helen liked Dr. Bell. He understood her signs. Dr. Bell told Helen's parents about a special school. It was the Perkins Institution for the Blind.

Helen's parents wrote to the Perkins school. The school said they had a teacher for Helen. The teacher was Anne Sullivan.

# Anne Sullivan

As a young girl, Anne Sullivan could not see well. She began going to the Perkins Institution for the Blind.

At the Perkins school, Anne met a woman named Laura Bridgman. Laura was blind and deaf.

Anne and other people "talked" to Laura using the manual alphabet. They signed letters on Laura's hand. The letters formed words. Laura felt the signs and understood the words.

Anne Sullivan (right) taught Helen (left) for many years.

After two operations, Anne got her sight back. She finished school and became Helen Keller's teacher. In 1887, Anne moved to Tuscumbia, Alabama. She planned to teach Helen the manual alphabet.

# Teaching Helen

Anne Sullivan worked with Helen Keller every day. She gave Helen a doll. Then, she signed the letters D-O-L-L on Helen's hand. Helen enjoyed repeating the signs on Anne's hand. But she did not understand what they meant.

One day, Anne and Helen went to the water pump. Helen put her hand in the running water. Anne signed W-A-T-E-R on Helen's hand. This time, Helen understood.

That day at the water pump changed Helen's life. She learned more and more words. Anne taught Helen to read raised letters. Helen learned to read and write.

Helen later became a talented writer.

Anne taught Helen to read braille, too. The braille alphabet is in raised dots. People read braille by feeling the dots. Helen enjoyed reading books in braille.

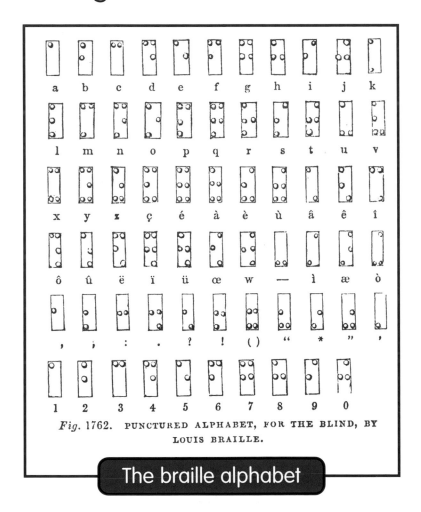

Fig. 1762. PUNCTURED ALPHABET, FOR THE BLIND, BY LOUIS BRAILLE.

The braille alphabet

# College Life

In 1898, Helen Keller and Anne Sullivan moved to Boston, Massachusetts. Helen became a student at the Cambridge School for Young Ladies.

Anne stayed by Helen's side. She told Helen what the teachers said. Helen was an excellent student.

In 1900, Helen Keller went to Radcliffe College. Back then, not many women went to college. Radcliffe was one of the few schools for women.

Helen took tests and got good grades. She wrote papers, too. Helen was good at writing. She began writing for a women's magazine. The magazine paid Helen to write the story of her life.

Helen studied at Radcliffe College for four years.

Helen's writings were later printed in a book. The book was called *The Story of My Life*. This book helped Helen become famous.

Helen graduated from Radcliffe with honors in 1904. She and Anne moved to Wrentham, Massachusetts. Helen wrote another book called *The World I Live In*. It was printed in 1908.

# Helping The Blind

Helen Keller took many speech lessons. In 1913, she gave her first speech. Helen gave speeches across the nation.

In 1924, Helen Keller began working with the American Foundation for the Blind. She raised money for them.

Helen won much support for the blind. She traveled to more than 25 countries. Helen met with lawmakers, too. Thanks to Helen, there are many U.S. laws that help the blind.

Helen met President Dwight D. Eisenhower and many other U.S. presidents.

Anne Sullivan died in 1936. Helen missed her teacher and best friend very much. Helen's secretary took over for Anne. Her name was Polly Thomson.

Helen wrote a book about Anne Sullivan. It was printed in 1955.

# Honoring Helen Keller

In 1964, President Lyndon B. Johnson gave Helen a special award. It was the Presidential Medal of Freedom. This medal is one of the highest United States honors.

President Lyndon B. Johnson

People around the world admire Helen Keller.

On June 1, 1968, Helen Keller died. Her funeral took place at the Washington National Cathedral.

Being blind and deaf did not stop Helen Keller from living a remarkable life. Her story gives hope to people around the world.

# More About Helen Keller

Helen often spoke out against war.

Helen fought for women's rights.

Helen acted in a movie about her life called *Deliverance*.

Helen wrote eight books.

*The Story of My Life* has been printed in more than 50 languages.

Helen learned to understand what people said by feeling their face as they spoke.

Helen visited soldiers who lost their sight in battle during World War II.

Helen knew Charlie Chaplin, Mark Twain, and other famous people.

During her life, Helen met 14 U.S. presidents.

# Important Dates

**June 27, 1880**  Helen Keller is born.

**1882**  Helen loses her sight and her hearing.

**1887**  Anne Sullivan begins teaching Helen.

**1898**  Helen begins studying at the Cambridge School for Young Ladies.

**1904**  Helen graduates from Radcliffe College with honors.

**1904**  Helen's first book is printed.

**1905**  Anne Sullivan marries John Macy.

**1924**  Helen begins working for the American Foundation for the Blind.

**1936**  Anne Sullivan Macy dies.

**1937**  Helen tours Japan.

**1955**  Helen writes a book about Anne Sullivan.

**June 1, 1968**  Helen Keller dies at the age of 87.

# Important Words

**braille** a system of writing for blind people that uses raised dots for letters.

**deaf** describes not being able to hear or to hear well.

**invent** to make something for the first time.

**manual alphabet** an alphabet in which letters are signed with hands and fingers.

**plantation** a large farm.

# Web Sites

**To learn more about Helen Keller,** visit ABDO Publishing Company on the World Wide Web at www.abdopub.com. Web sites about Helen Keller are featured on our Book Links page. These links are routinely monitored and updated to provide the most current information available.

# Index